WHOLESIGHT
THE SPIRIT QUEST

by
FREDERICK PARKER-RHODES
Pendle Hill Pamphlet 217

About the Author/Born 1914 of well-to-do parents, this British Friend led an unstressful childhood. His main interest was acquiring knowledge, an interest which has remained with him ever since, though increasingly balanced by the spiritual quest and by a delight in friendships. He took an unprotesting part in world War II as a government scientist. For many years attracted to communism, he became disillusioned with its want of Wholesight and Stalin's purges. In 1948, along with his wife, Damaris, he joined the Society of Friends where, as he puts it, "one can worship God without scorning those who worship other gods or none." His professional interests include fungi, linguistics, and theoretical physics, all loosely connected by mathematics. Among Quakers he has been more concerned with deepening the spiritual life than with good works. To date he has three surviving children and one grandchild.

"The present pamphlet," he writes, "gathers up some of the threads of my abiding concern for Wholesight, in the belief that this is the most urgent need of man today. If we cannot find coherence among religion, science, art, and politics, all these will come to nothing."

Request for permission to quote or to translate should be addressed to Pendle Hill Publications, Wallingford, Pennsylvania 19086.

Copyright © 1978 by Pendle Hill
ISBN 0-87574-217-3

Library of Congress catalog card number 77-95406

Printed in the United States of America by
Sowers Printing Company, Lebanon, Pennsylvania
February 1978: 2,500

SOME PHILOSOPHERS now argue that one can say nothing rational about the Whole of what is. An equally onesided opinion is that whatever may be said about a part, in disregard of its being a part, is bound to be partial, and so falls short of the truth. Either view is mistaken: one can talk sense enough about both the whole and its parts, provided one doesn't overestimate the extent of man's present knowledge. We stand today overburdened with bits and pieces, useful for our immediate purposes but with little relevance for the long term strategy that we now need. In short we have, to an alarming degree, lost sight of the Whole.

Two difficulties stand in the way of Wholesight. One is the reliance we place on the kind of logic we have used during our long quest for control of the pieces. We never question that Yes denies No: that if any proposition is true, its contradiction must needs be false. Yet whenever such a clear contradiction presents itself, there will be some level in the Whole where Yes and No can peacefully coexist in the shelter of a wider comprehension.

The second difficulty is the other side of the same coin. For our simple-minded logic has taken away our understanding of the language of Wholesight, which is the language of myth, of poetry, of art, of music. We still admire their beauty, but discount their wisdom, fearing that wisdom itself may be betrayed by such a medium. We are right to be wary of insights inherited from ages of ignorance: even Wholesight gains from a knowledge of the parts. But those who recognized Wholesight as their supreme goal had something to say which is no longer said, and none are better qualified than they to teach us to recapture it.

The problem is to weave together the objective approach of science with the subjective vision of the arts. If religion is the name we give to their offspring, it must be a humbler creature than usually bears that title. True religion dictates neither to science nor to art, for the whole truth includes its parts harmoniously; the tree does not fly, for its roots are in the earth, nor does it need to, for its crown is in heaven. Subjective creativity seeks a process which all may delight in, if they have a taste for the work and share the goals of the artist; science seeks for truths which all may verify, if they have the needed skills and access to the same area of experience. These two are complementary, but without Wholesight they can seem enemies, and the advance of science has led to quarrels which are still to be healed. This matter is too weighty to be left to those who take sides. We need Wholesight now, more urgently than these disputants will admit.

My aim, therefore, is to show by myths and stories how we may gain a little fluency in that forgotten tongue. I give no references—that is no part of this discipline—and I adhere to no text, for variation, addition, invention, are essential parts of the method.

I Creation Is Circular

The Whole has no boundaries. So if, as in many mythologies, we talk of a beginning and an end, we must remember that the beginning is the end, and is chosen only to fit the story. Time, too, is often itself a symbol of eternity—the eternity of the naked now—for real time is not the unbreakable framework that it seems, but is only a part, beyond which there are many things in the Whole not subject to it. Ultimately the circle of creation is unbroken, without beginning and without end.

The want of a starting point puts one in mind of the old conundrum about the hen and the egg. Neither can be said to come before the other. But hens are many, though the Whole is one. And what about the cocks, which have no place in the parable? What we seek is something a little different: a bird that is unique and parthogenetic.

The Phoenix

There is but one Phoenix, and one is the Egg she lays. She flies from the world's end to roost in the magical tragacanth tree which grows nowhere, in no land, on no planet. This is her song: "I was tomorrow, I am today, and yesterday I shall be still." She builds her nest in the tragacanth tree, a nest of fragrant foliage and resin-bearing twigs. When all is perfect and in order she lays in it the Egg. She carries fire from the heart of the true sun into that nest. It smokes, then, with a sweet smelling smoke which there is none to delight in. It burns and crackles and bursts at last into fierce flames. The Phoenix, sacred and imperishable, brooding her Egg by herself, sacrifices herself, to herself, in the dawn hour that no time tells. That is why what is, is what it is. She burns utterly away in that great fire, but the tree is not consumed. On it rests still the Egg, woken by destruction into life, incubated in the heat of its mother's death, hatched in the dying embers. Then the young Phoenix, which is the old Phoenix, breaks full fledged from the empty shell. She flies forthwith to the world's end, till the time that is beyond time returns as the dawning of time—now and forever, world without end.

This briefly told tale has acquired though the ages a multitude of meanings. Some find the core of it in the cosmic egg: visible world as Egg, invisible creator as the Phoenix; which brings forth that which is out of that which is not. Others see a contrast between the formless absolute of the smooth, rounded Egg and the visible world of forms—the Phoenix, most beautiful of birds. Some again say that the egg means matter, which flowers into Spirit as the Egg hatches into the Phoenix, symbol of Spirit, the end of matter. Christian writers find an echo of Paul's concept of the thrice reflexive sacrifice of God in Christ on the cross—by himself, of himself, to himself. But if you look too analytically you are likely to miss the point. A crystal of quartz has many faces, but it is none the less one crystal; in the same way, all these interpretations are truly there, but each by itself is a diminishment, even a betrayal, of the whole.

Most importantly the Phoenix and the Egg demonstrate that creation is to be seen as circular. This does not refer to a cycle of time. It is not an endlessly repeated event, even though that is what it reduces to on third hand reporting. The myth itself makes this plain enough, but it is nevertheless a very difficult idea to get across. That is why I urge you to forget time. God created time. He gave it a starting point but no finishing point, *and* then He went on to create other things. The core and kernel of our quest is the "and then." Once created, time continues forever, but the "ever after" is only a part of the Whole. We, prisoners of time, are baffled by eternity; but time is nothing in our Father's kingdom, and it is false to think of it as enclosing all that is.

This is the commonest, but by no means the only, misapprehension one may have in the reading of myths. Another is to insist on some kind of causal nexus. You can't tell a story which doesn't deal with causation, but myths are stories not to be taken literally but intuitively. Causality is a concept of science, largely irrelevant beyond the limits of the scientists' tunnel vision. The relation between the Phoenix and her Egg is that of interdependence. The beginning depends on the end, and the end (not a ceasing to be, but a revealed intention) depends on the beginning. Indeed, no part of the Whole can be thought of except in dependence on the rest of it. There is nothing high if nothing else is low; nothing is good if there is no evil; nothing goes before if nothing follows. There is no Egg if there is none to lay it.

The Stair of Bethel

Once, in the days before history began, Jacob, namefather of Israel, was wandering in the wideness of the land of Canaan. An ancient land was this, replete already with ancestral legends and with ruins long since abandoned to the storied beasts. Benighted, the namefather lay down and dreamed dreams in his sleep. It was in the morning of mankind, when earth and heaven were one world. A mighty stairway reached up to the radiance above—a flight of form-laid steps, on whose top was heaven built. All the levels of being were plain to see, each resting snugly on the one beneath, the highest of all bearing the invisible spendor. Up and down on this great stair angels passed, so much was that dream world one. When Jacob awoke, in awe and wonder he called the place Bethel, God's abode—as men do still.

Of anything in the Whole we may ask: what is its substance, and what is its form? Are these inseparable, or is the form a thing in its own right? Most of the things we see about us are mere static shapes; but some forms have a life of their own. Waves on the sea ceaselessly move over the surface, without shifting the water from its place; but if it were not for the water we would see no form. The flame of a candle stays perched like a bird on a bush, but its substance, the burning wax, is perpetually renewed from the candle below.

Living creatures, too, are fluent forms which renew their substance, albeit more slowly. There are forms in the world whose substance is found in the forms of the preceding step. The life of a beehive is such. Each bee is itself a form imposed fluently on a transitory store of matter. But the colony of bees is a form imposed on the whole collection of bees, whereby they work wonderfully together for the continuation of the whole. The way in which the colony maintains itself is wholly different from the way the individual forms are kept in being (do not be deceived by those who liken a beehive to an "organism"), but it is still a form, two steps removed from inanimate matter. So, too, are the multifarious ways of men— but with this difference, that our social structures, mirrored in our minds, support yet further levels which have no parallels, so far as we yet know, among the insects.

Where does it all end? How many steps make up the Stair of Bethel? How far is it from earth to heaven? Of course, we can't really know. If it were an infinite number, either the circle of creation would not be closed, as the Phoenix tells us it is, or the Stair would become a smooth ramp. But to set a particular number of steps would be outrunning knowledge. The physical and organic levels, being both below us, are well known to science; about these we can have no doubts. Still less can we doubt our own human level, where our wonderings begin, and which our wanderings hardly ever leave. All religions teach the paramount importance of the level beyond, that of the Spirit—but many people nowadays will have none of that. Mystical tradition tells of others, such as the Christian Trinity and the Hindu absolute. But we must remember that the Stair is an imperfect image. There is neither top nor bottom to the Whole. What is above heaven is below earth; the circle of creation is unbroken and complete.

The Sky and the Tree

It came, the Seed, from the high forest's eaves, flickered through the ambient air, and landed on the soft and naked earth, a token to our Mother of our Father's love. The ready rains of heaven washed it well in, planting an intention in the causal soil. This seed held within it certain instructions—handed down, with countless amendments, through God-weary ages—and it followed them minutely. The first root grew towards the lifeless darkness, and began to feed in the humus. Then two leaves unfolded to the sun, and grew green with chlorophyll to capture the light of life. Came the first snows, and it had grown and shed a little crop of leaves, had begun to ramify its rootlets through the soil.

All the while the face of heaven smiled and frowned: sometimes bright with sunshine, sometimes wreathed in mists, sometimes with great gales, sometimes with gentle rain. As a cause flowers in its consequence, so this Tree grew, year by year. It was an Ash—*Fraxinus excelsior*. The tall trunk stood midmost in Middle-earth. The greenleaf crown spread through the halls of heaven, song-bright sanctuary of birds. The Tree held heaven and earth in one embrace—which is what trees are for.

Thus was the purpose of heaven obediently fulfilled. Then men came, with fire and axe, and cut it down. Its tale was ended before its time was told, and the forest floor was cleared for the patient ploughs. The ancient dance of cause and consequence cut short, new processes began their play. And this also was the purpose of heaven. The sun, the wind, the rain blessed men's fields as they had blessed the growing Ash. And now there came a word from God by the mouth of the prophet to teach man, too, to turn towards heaven, planting in his causal heart a new Seed, charged with instructions for a new and more than vegetable life.

The quarrel between science and religion consists in this, that religion teaches that God is the first cause, from whom proceeds the spiritual, human, and still lower orders of being, whereas science finds that things have gone the other way. From physical matter life arises; from animal life humanity has evolved, imposing new and subtler forms on animal material; and, if there is anything beyond, that too, must be a form subsisting on substances of an earlier level.

Wholesight requires that mutually exclusive hypotheses must both be entertained, and a framework of thought found in which they may coexist. Here the framework is not far to seek. In the religious image of God's creation "high" and "low" represent an ordering by purpose, each end being "higher" than the means by which it is attained: in scientific metaphor effects are held to "arise" from their causes. both agree on which trend is "upwards." The only clash is about the order in time. But as religious thinking treats time metaphorically, this is a trivial disagreement. It doesn't really mean "first" when it says "first;" it means "last": God is Omega, not Alpha.

Once again we must remember the Phoenix. Creation is circular, and every level within the Whole is both the first and the last. Teleologically the existence of God requires each lower level. There is Spirit, therefore there must be human society; society calls into being the animal substance of humanity; animals postulate matter, and matter the unstructured absolute.

This is why the angels on the Stair of Bethel go both up and down, some bringing God's will to men, some carrying the effects of earthly causes into higher planes. Do not deride any wisdom for being contrary to your own: and do not overestimate your tools—"It's not in the Bible," "It's not demonstrable"—for much in the Whole is neither.

It is a flaw in the tale of the tree that it fails to present the creation process as circular. There is no first cause, nor final purpose either—no universal apotheosis. Goal succeeds goal till the beginning comes round again; man's needs superseding the tree's needs is only a single nudge of the wheel of the world. Our trouble is that we think of most of the wheel as missing, since it is beyond our narrow logic. But seen fully and in the round there is no gap—how can there be gaps in the Whole? Time has a beginning, if not, perhaps an end. Yet what is time but a streamer in the hand of the Divine Dancer, tracing the figures of creation for us creatures to wonder at?

II *Entry into the Human State*

This, then, is the setting for man's story. We stand on the third step above the formless absolute. Human life, with its fluent forms carried in the minds of rational beings, is unlikely to be unique in the cosmos; but its evolution has depended on so many fortunate accidents that it cannot be other than rare. Spiritual life probably needs even more exacting conditions— an intervention, perhaps, from its own future, a trick of time impossible at an earlier level, and even now all too liable to miscarry. We are nevertheless invited, even pressed, to enter the Commonwealth of Heaven. We may perhaps picture this next level as the furthest of all from the absolute: from here the way may lead down hill again. But the hazards before us are great.

The Feast

Gone was the Age of Gold. The last ruler of that magical era lived all alone in a vast palace, served by familiars conjured by sorcery from the Void. They told him that the Lord of the Void planned to invade his lands; and they advised him to consult the people about it—people whom he never saw, for they belonged to a different age from his. To induce them to come to the palace he planned a feast. When all was ready he sent his magical messengers to invite the chief men of the nation to come to it. But they cared nothing for the Survivor—as they called their king—and they all made excuses.

Hearing this, the king said, "If the leaders and great men despise me, I shall call the beggars and vagabonds instead." So he sent out his messengers again, to invite all the social outcasts. These came gladly. When they had enjoyed the feast the king said, "My palace is empty, and all the castles of the land are unmanned. You, who have come to my feast, are to be the new rulers of the people, to lead them against the Lord of the Void."

But that Lord knew that his Void could prevail only against the non-existent. So he called off the invasion.

If human-level life is a rare thing in the universe, it might well be that the difficult step from this order to the next will never be accomplished, leaving the spiritual level forever empty. It must have been so in the beginning. This is why the vast palace is represented as empty—at least of human beings. When the story opens we have not yet received the summons to the feast.

Outside the palace there are people, aspirants in principle to the spiritual order. But there is also the Void: the inhuman and unspiritual environment in which of necessity we live, needing for our existence the animal and inanimate substances which it provides. The Void perpetually threatens the precarious experiment of the spiritual life. Without the human souls on which the forms of Spirit feed, there is indeed no Spirit, any more than there are waves on the dry oceans of Mars. If no one heeds the invitation to the feast, the Void without will indeed triumph over the nothingness within, and all our tedious progress come to nothing.

It would be no very extraordinary thing if that were so. It is a strange invitation we are offered: an entertainment beyond the frontiers of the known world, to a place whose existence most of us doubt, from a host who is suspected of being the fantasy of diseased or uneducated minds. Who *would* be interested? Cranks and crackpots, one would suppose—and those with nothing to lose.

For it was not the top people but the bottom people that came to the feast. Why not? Something to eat, and at least a tale to tell back home. But this "new rulers" bit—what would they make of that? We aren't told how they reacted. One wonders if there was that much to react to, anyway. No doubt the old order carried on as before, never noticing the new grass growing under their feet. When the life drains away from a place it is a slow process, and not very painful.

So we need not fear that there will be no takers for the Kingdom of Heaven. But everyone must ask, really doubting, can I come? Or do I in my heart write it off as a fraud? The twist is, there's no possible way of knowing that it isn't.

Theseus

Before the Eruption, when the Atlanteans still had power over the world, Minos their king used to receive from Athens a tribute of teen-agers to be trained for the bull-dance. At the great sacrifice for Poseidon the Earthquaker they were turned over to the Bull King. Few survived, and none ever got home.

One year, when the lots were cast, Theseus the prince was among those chosen. It was in the butchers' quarter that he spent his last days at home. During his training in Knossos he caught the fancy of Ariadne, Minos's daughter, who promised to help him escape. Their plan was to kill the Bull King, who dwelt, sacred and furious, in a labyrinth beyond the wit of strangers. So Theseus had from Ariadne a hank of wool, by paying out which he could avoid false turnings. One night, with this, a lamp, and his butcher's knife, he entered the labyrinth, and after hours of wandering came face to face with the Bull King, strong and desperate, but dazzled by the lamp. Skilled with the knife, Theseus quickly did what he'd come for, and returned without mishap, following his thread.

It was soon known, and the people panicked—for this was sacrilege, meriting the Earthquaker's vengeance. In the commotion Theseus, with his Athenian friends and Ariadne, escaped to Herakleia and set sail for home. To kill the root is to kill the tree, and soon after the Bull King's slaughter Poseidon did indeed end the baneful Atlantean power, in ashfall and darkness and huge tidal waves.

This is an ancient Greek tale, the one only explicitly set in the time before the Greeks took over the Minoan empire. This was for them the dream time, when the world was in the making, and all-time precedents were laid down. The precedents were weighty, and for us they are three—those three things that Theseus took with him into the labyrinth: the knife, the lamp, and the hank of wool.

The knife stands for technical competence; the lamp represents clear thought. Both are important. Although I am here pointing out the path to Wholesight through the medium of imagination, parable, and allusion, we must not suppose that rational thinking can be set aside. But the important item for us is the ball of wool. This stands for discipline, commitment, patience, and the humility to correct mistakes. Patience and humility are both parts of discipline, but this word has a deeper meaning than mere obedience and perseverance: it is a necessary corrective to the freedom of the Spirit, the intoxication which always threatens those who accept the invitation to the feast.

It is all too clear how few among us have this gift of discipline, how few possess the thread which lets them answer that of God in everyone they meet. Those who lack it must, in Paul's words, test the spirits, and take conscious care to resist impulses which those more disciplined might blindly avoid. It is a thread which lets one retrace every step and undo one's errors, not a set of rules which makes one infallible. The price of infallibility is a rigour which blocks the life-giving approaches of the Spirit. For Spirit is a living form which needs perpetually to renew her substance, and whatever resists change is soon left lifeless behind her. The world had never known such righteous men as those Pharisees whom Jesus slated. But their glory was written in their books, not in their hearts, and the wind danced over them, seeking her sustenance in new nations.

Prometheus

In the beginning gods and men lived side by side, gods on the mountain tops and men in the valleys. The one mark by which one might know a god was that he understood the mystery of fire. Naturally, this aroused envy among men, for they knew that it was good, and they did not have it. Now there was one who championed their cause whose name was Prometheus, son of Japhet. They said therefore to Promethus, "Fetch us this fire." and he agreed, and devised a plan to do it.

One day when the gods were at a feast, he climbed their sacred mountain. He found no one about, except a minor god called Erythros, who had been left to tend the hearths while the rest were merrymaking. "Never has so ill a thing befallen," said Prometheus, "for the fire of the feast has failed! Therefore the high gods have sent me to fetch fire." "Who then are you?" asked Erythros. "Who would they send but Logios, of course, the butt of Olympus? and what's more, disguised as a mortal for their sport!"

Erythros, quite taken in, gave him a brand from the hearth. Now Prometheus might with this token have joined the gods and been accepted as one of them; but that was not his purpose. Instead, with the brand in his mouth, he made all speed down the mountain to his friends below. Then he taught them how to use and tend the fire. Everyone from then on had his own flame, and they were like gods. The holy mountain was thereafter fenced about, and they saw the gods no longer face to face.

When the trick was discovered Zeus, father of gods, cursed Prometheus. And this was his punishment, that he should see the ugliness of his entrails day after day, and never again know peace and rest. He was chained on Mount Ararat to the Rock of Knowledge, where every day a vulture came, and tore open his belly and feasted on his liver. Some told that he was eventually rescued by Herakles, who carried him to the Isles of Ever-youth; others later gave the credit to Christ at his Harrowing of Hell. But that is another story.

Unlike the story of Theseus, this tale has no historical setting. Whereas Theseus slew a monster, Prometheus acquired a treasure, a divine talisman which is also a fundamental item in man's technical armory. The myth also has a feast symbolizing the spiritual order. But here no outsiders are invited in. Prometheus' task is to bring down a gift of the Spirit to men, not to seize it for himself.

What gift from heaven is best for man is a point on which many differ. Buddha brings knowledge of the cause of suffering, which is desiring; Jesus brings knowledge of the cause of happiness, which is loving. Prometheus goes back further, for his gift, according to some early commentators, is speech. So the myth of Prometheus is about our first entry into the human state. But when the commentators say "speech" they mean not that which made men out of apes, but the oracular and exalted utterance of the poet and mystic. This the myth calls "fire" because, like fire, it destroys; and what it destroys is our ancient innocence.

For, as with Adam's magic apple, there came a curse with this stolen fire: the language of self-knowledge. By the light of the stolen fire one may see the nature of theft, by telling lies one may learn the wickedness of false words. This was the ugliness revealed on the Rock of Knowledge, and from that day forward it has followed those of us who take words seriously. We are the talking creatures, adding to our animal nature the supernature of speech, and reason, the daughter of speech. The human form is not coded in our chromosomes, but lives in our hearts in the shifting and fallible attempts to read

God's will: our values, laws, habits, taboos which our children learn after us and do not scruple to amend. Speech is the medium of our humanity.

But talking is not only to show us our shadows but to build up, to instruct. Jesus gave almost nothing but items of ethical instruction. Ages come when these precepts lose their force, and have to be tested to destruction. The whole system is taken to pieces, and the reasons behind the traditions revealed—or demolished—by disobedience. Ours is such an age. It is a Promethean age, exulting in desperate adventures. Our hope lies in discipline, that frayed thread whereby we need not be thrown back to our beginnings, but emerge from each experiment a little more safely human, a step nearer the Redemption which is the Christian hope.

III   The Spirit Quest: Destiny and Duty

The purpose of human life is to be the basis for the life of the Spirit. Human lives, like animal lives, come to an end, but there is a life which is eternal, the life of spiritual form. This life is called "eternal" not because it goes on forever, but because it is not tied to the order of events in time. It has its own way of ending, for it is the substance of levels beyond it; but the hardest crossing is that between the human and the spiritual. This is our destiny. Not destiny only, but duty. To make the great transition from natural to spiritual is the collective task for all mankind, which we can evade only at the cost of being abandoned by the dancing waves and driving wind, as the animals are abandoned in death. We have been created to be used as material for a higher being: one of the steps of the Stair of Bethel, every one of which is necessary for the existence of the highest.

The Spirit is our purpose, as we are one of the purposes of

that animal life which underlies our humanity, and which we must cherish, in our own interest, lest we ourselves perish from the earth. We are to rule the earth—not ravish it—as heaven rules us, not by compulsion but by allurement. By learning to be a worthy purpose, to crown the animal creation with kindness rather than cruelty, to greet our fellow beings with reverence rather than rapine, we prepare for the Commonwealth of Heaven. The Holy Spirit is a fluent form which plays with our souls as the wind plays with the sea. We can hinder her play with ice-floes of pride and breakwaters of self-regard, we can refuse to sway with the wind, we can stand stiff and dumb amid the dancing of heaven—or we can trust ourselves to be blown away, safe in God's love, to the garden of delight.

But where and what is this garden? The world we know is not only imperfect; it is implanted with seeds of its own destruction, while the seeds of goodness are sown among brambles and thorns. How can one rhapsodize about the dancing of heaven?

The Holy Grail

The first of beings was born of Ocean. He lived beside the sea and was called Fisherman. He found a wife in a cave of the cliff; she was called Fruitful, and she fed him on sea fruit from a lordly dish. They had many children, myth-shadows before the gods, who had from their father the wealth of wisdom, and from their mother the milk of love. Youngest of the myth-shadows was Harvester. He taught his brothers to work, to eat earth born things, and he cut the crops which they sowed. His wish was to be ever the youngest. He lay in wait with his scythe, and when his father came home he robbed him of his pintle. Thus the long winter began. Fisherman fled with

Fruitful to the world's end, where they lived in a castle of glass, powerless but plentifully fed from their inexhaustible dish.

All else in the world was Harvester's, but the loss of this one treasure he could not forget. He, too, had many children, and the youngest was Japhet, father of men. He it was who passed on the empty memory of Wholesight to his descendants. It became a mystery among men. They called it the Holy Grail, but what manner of thing it was no one knew. For some it was Ceridwen's magic cauldron; for some, Christ's cup of the Last Supper; and many things else for others.

One spring in King Arthur's time—those nine years when history gave place to weightier matters—there came to court a sage who claimed knowledge of the Grail and how it might be won. Advised by Merlin the loremaster, the king asked the visitor, "What skills and honors can you claim?" Replied the sage, "I am a master of the Kabbala, the Tarot, the I Ching, Alchemy, Astrology, and much else besides." This answer led Arthur to doubt his worth; but he let him set out, with arms and a mount. Months after, word came that his body had been found. At that time the Eastern Emperor's son was at court. He said, "Surely I, heir to the Empire, will find this Grail." So he, too, was given leave, and before long there was weeping in Byzantium.

Next came a peasant lad, claiming knighthood if he should succeed. Roughly clothed, he had nothing of value but a torc, a neck ring of twisted copper, which his mother had told him was his father's token. All at court laughed at him, and would not let him in. At this the king was angry, saying, "Which of you, then, dares the quest?" So several of the knights in shame set out. Not all died, but none succeeded. When eight of the nine years were gone, and hope was fading, Percival the peasant came again. And this time Arthur insisted that he should go. While proud knights jeered, he rode out, wobbling on his high horse.

On the Western road he fell in with an affable stranger, and asked, "Which way to the Grail Castle?" The stranger answered readily, "Right at the next fork, second left after the ford. It isn't far, and you can't miss it." But it was, and he did, wandering many days in the forest before he saw a new painted sign, "To the Grail Castle." But a fog came up, and darknesss, and again many days passed fruitlessly. Back on the road at last he met with another rider. They went on together, and soon became fast friends. Percival learned many things, for this was a loremaster. He was therefore sad at heart when this friend fell ill. Arriving at a mountain monastery half way to heaven the friend said, "Leave me here. Go learn what you can, and return in three days."

Percival next met an old woman, who said she had skill in healing. Told of his sick friend, she promised to visit him—but himself she warned to make haste before the floodwaters came. He hurried on therefore, and reached the river. There was a boatman, who had just come over, saying there would be no more crossings that year. So!—too late, and the three days gone, and his promise not kept. "Keep Faith," the boatman called, and pushed out into the racing water. After a bitter night the river again flowed sweet and slow, and the old boatman was back. Percival recognized his friend, who could scarce hearten him to make the crossing.

Over the river they met a girl travelling their way, whom Percival hoisted up behind him. They saw a castle standing on a high hill, and he asked the girl who held it. "They say it's the dwelling of King Fisherman," she said. In all haste Percival rode up the hill, never heeding that his friend did not follow. He tolled the great bell at the gate. A sullen porter looked out and without a word struck the bell thrice, at which seven armed knights rode forth. Percival made all speed back to the road. As he passed his friend called out, "Keep Hope"—but the girl said, "Hurry, they're after us!" Not till nightfall did he stop for weariness, and then on an impulse took off his father's token and gave it to the girl; she thanked him wryly. They slept on the ground that night. But come sunrise girl and horse were gone. So he set off on foot, and soon met his friend coming to meet him. "Keep Love," was all he said, and took him up on his own horse. Some days after they came upon a fine charger, in kingly style harnessed, grazing alone by the roadside. "Here we part," said his friend, "this is your horse to ride to the world's end."

So Percival rode off into the rain wet evening, all alone. He was in no hurry now, so disappointments didn't distress him. He was not proud, so slights didn't hurt him. He was not well informed, so he didn't hesitate to question. He was not brave, and wasted no strength in fighting. Thus it was he came safe to the world's end.

And here, only a cable's length across the sea's dead calm, rose the castle, high walled and silent. On the ebb, he went up, but all seemed empty and unmanned. He shouted, but had no answer. He called, "Let me in, for peace is my pleasure. If war be your welcome, come out!" Still no answer but "Out!" on the fringe of hearing. He came close to the wall, and peering, saw a knight within, armed as he was. He drew his sword, and so did the other. Blow for blow they fought, till sword was blunt and arm exhausted. He had turned his heel on this latest unsuccess when, astonishingly, he found himself inside the castle—its walls all of glass, its people majestic and silent. Before him a slow procession passed, at its tail a fine woman with a great golden dish. Following, he came into a vast chamber, in it a bed translucently curtained. Here lay an aged king, pale and purple sheeted, so old and ill that Percival could not but ask, "What sickness has his Majesty?"

The old king answered, "I am robbed of my virtue by Harvester, my son, and lie here these many thousand years, waiting for one to ask that question." "How come that a god be gelded?" "Anything may come," said the king, "if no one wonders at it. Wonderment is the framework of the world, and by your wondering I am whole again." So saying he got up, and put his arms round Percival: "Your quest is nearly done. This is, indeed, the Holy Grail you see. I give it, gladly and in gratitude, to your lord King Arthur. One thing only you have yet to do. Go now!" At this the great doors on the further side of the chamber opened, and Percival passed through.

Thus he returned, unjourneyed, to Arthur's hall. The knights were at table, and the sparrows flew through the rafters. Arthur was with them, and Merlin beside him. "Keep awake," said the loremaster. The king rose, saying "Welcome, Sir Percival! Here is a token which you thought not to see again." Percival took the outheld copper torc, and put it round his neck; and Merlin's face fell. Then the king asked, "What do you bring us from the world's end, what soul food to heal the sickness of mankind?" In answer the hero passed around the company, wordlessly serving each from the inexhaustible dish. All but their watchmen who, as he finished, ran in crying, "Arm you for battle: the host of Mordor is in sight!" Percival set down the Grail and went with the rest to war, before they'd heard what he might have said to prevent them.

Arthur did not return. Those who survived were scattered; and their kingly hall, with the Grail in it, was never seen afterwards. As for Percival, he stayed in Britain as long as King Constantine reigned, but when Maelgwn seized power, he crossed over to Brittany. There he became a monk under Gildas the Wise, and was notable for his austerities. When he died they found round his neck the torc of twisted copper. Gildas said, "See now, brothers, why he failed, who so nearly succeeded." He told the monks to bury it with him. Little did he know how much more than burial it would need.

The Golden Age—the most attractive and insidious of all myths—when men were innocent, happy, and whole, reflects the durability of our happy memories and the delibility of sorrows. I see my first days on earth as mankind in general has seen its original condition, wiped clean from irksome blemishes. It is useless for historians to tell us that in reality our ancestors were brutal, ignorant, and ringed with fear. We know that very well, but how can we believe it, when we have forgotten how it felt?

Christians attribute the loss of Eden to man's discovery of the difference between good and evil. Before there was ethical instruction there were no ethics, and no wickedness was done, for there was none to call it wicked. But as soon as instruction began, disobedience began, too. Freedom to belong to the Commonwealth of Heaven is the same freedom by which we enter the Competition for Hell. There is great truth in the Eden myth. The sin of Adam is the inherent ability to sin, which is the birthright of humankind. If that were taken from us, we would be shut out from all spiritual adventure. But good people always wish it were not so. They want it to be harder to do evil than to do good; they want to believe that the Redemption of man by Jesus might save them from evil. They want to run away from the bad people, not stay and redeem them. They want to find the Holy Grail and keep it in a cupboard, for fear it should get spoilt, or smashed by yahoos.

The search for Wholesight is not for the learned, not for the power wielders, not for the brave. It is a task for those without ambition, for no ambition will be served by it. Nor is this a quest for the moralist: Wholesight makes no one good, and may even lead to loving unworthy folk, and standing off from saints. And what is this Wholesight anyway? It's what we had in the Golden Age, before all our troubles began—a time which never was.

We are like climbers who have reached a high pass in the

morning. Westwards lies a rare and ruby land, covered in cloud. That's where we've come from. But we forget the teeming and terrible jungle that lies under the clouds. Eastwards we can see nothing for the glare of the rising sun; but by evening there, too, will be the indescribable beauty, and by that time, if we press on with our journey, we shall have arrived there. We are right to forget what we shall not see again; we are right to remember the thing which has never yet been. We were brutes, without sight; we are men, and partly seeing but, with the gift of Wholesight, immortal spirits we shall become.

As a theme of mythology the quest goes back to remote antiquity. The great treasure guarded by fearsome monsters in a far country makes a good story line, as well as being an apt simile for the hidden wisdom of Wholesight. But there is also the theme of the Precious Bane, which has been unaccountably neglected. Though not strictly the first, Tolkien's *Lord of the Rings* is the only example known to most readers.

I have therefore introduced this theme into my version of the Grail story. For there are things we need to lose, as well as things to find. What things? Pride is one. Growth economics, the true sacrament of pride, is another. But there is a deeper and more precious bane: that self-sufficiency that man delights in and of which no animal has ever dreamt. Not only the lonely survivalism of the pioneer, not only the self-counfidence of the careerist, but the collective assumption that our species, after millions of years of evolution, has at last reached a condition in which our life can be an end in itself. In short, the faith of the humanist, for whom there is no level beyond the human. This is the Piscean heresy which the Aquarian age anathematizes.

And why is this bane so precious? Because it is the seal of

our humanity. The humanist way of life is possible, at least on a limited scale. All that is needed is to refuse to go any further, and perfect our own little garden, a showpiece in the wilderness of the world. And the cost? Only now can we begin to reckon up the cost—and that is, no doubt, why the Precious Bane theme seems so recently discovered. All that belongs to the spiritual level in human life is what we must pay. All the works of creative imagination will lose their force: poetry, music, art, and the free answering of the spirit in love and grace, all these which represent yet higher peaks to climb will become empty forms without meaning. The gift of free will, that built-in paradox of humanity, will turn to mere unpredictability, and in due course be restrained by law, a public danger. There will be no purpose left in life.

But there is also a price to be paid for giving up this baneful treasure. Millions must die because our planet cannot sustain them. For the rational behavior this wild hope depends on is not forthcoming, nor ever will be so long as anyone is still allowed to go their own way. But the cost of return is finite, while the cost of going on is infinite: either total material loss, which is the more likely, or total spiritual loss. The choice is ours which it will be, unless we can break ourselves of this pride.

The positive quest, like the negative, is not for the proud. We can win wholesight, not by cleverness, but by magic. Coincidence has to make do for fortitude, and serendipity for certitude. And these things do not work for those who carry their father's token. Those who desire to be ends in themselves do not experience meaningful coincidences. But those who are content to be people for others find that things happen which they can be happy with. The very same things, perhaps, which the proud just can't stand.

Hope we must have, however hopeless. When things go well we must not doze in the slumber of smugness, nor despair when things go ill. We must carry our seeking even to the end of the world. The Holy Grail is not to be found by any who have not sought till their strength fails.

It is kept in a glass castle. When you reach the world's end and find nothing, you turn round, defeated—and you're there! Your own soul is the castle, your own consciousness its glassy wall. What psychologists call the "unconscious" stands open to all who have lost the fear of themselves. All of us have terrible things inside of us which it is not absurd to fear. But what Christians call the "forgiveness of sins," or the "grace of God," is freely offered to each of us. To know that our nasty corners do not shut us off from love, that imperfections are allowed for in God's plan for us, is to overcome the self-horror from which so many people suffer.

In the glass castle we find a world of echoes and reflections. Everybody one meets there is oneself, everything one hears is one's own voice. At first it will seem a hall of distorting mirrors. But little by little the fragmentary echoes and partial reflections will merge into a picture of the whole self. And when it is fully clear we shall find that we are back home. Everything will be utterly ordinary once more, but now we know that it is ordinary because is is our own home, not because we have lost the springtime newness of the child's vision.

He who completes the double quest—the quest for what we must lose as well as what we must win—becomes a redeemer. Christian dogma says that Christ is the Redeemer, suggesting that there is none other. But in Mahayana Buddhism there is the Bodhisattva, one who, having attained enlightenment, rejects the privilege of entering Nirvana and opts instead to continue in the world, helping others along the way. These souls are therefore redeemers, and their ideal a noble one.

This is not an image we meet in the more familiar versions of the Grail story, where the hero merely witnesses a vision of the Risen Christ. So our Grail Hero, Percival, stops short of full success. But this, too, has a meaning, for the redemption of the world, though certainly begun, is yet more certainly incomplete. There is a place in our mythography for a failed Redeemer. The true redeemer not only completes his quest, but leads others into it, and out again, teaching what he has learned, and learning what others have to teach. He is not aloof from the human scene, but more thoroughly integrated than others, coming not as Lord but as servant.

Above all, the redeemer must help in healing the world's ill. This is the climax of the positive quest. It is wonder that makes a healer, just as surprise is the seal of the prophet. Charlatans and tricksters have nothing to be surprised at. Wonder is what we don't expect, what lies outside our current mental set. To have no faculty of wonder is to have no idea what things happen according to laws. Without this sense of the marvellous our experience would congeal into an unending commonplace. As soon as the commonplace begins to astonish you, you can begin to understand. And when, at last, you *have* understood, when you *have* gained Wholesight, when you have passed through spiritual adolescence and become a citizen of the Heavenly Commonwealth—you must not sleep. That is, you must not abandon your gifts.

"They who know," says the Dao-de-jing, "do not speak: they who speak do not know." This is true, but if it were the whole truth who would learn? There is a place for speech as well as a higher place for silence. Quakers learn much of the spiritual Way in their silent meetings; but one can be famished for words, and in those times speech is in order. The would-be redeemer who neglects the needs of the wordy world is false to his trust. His wisdom dies with him, and no one is any the wiser for his passing. Information exists only in transit, and few indeed are those who can tap the impalpable telepathic circuits of the spirit world. Even though poetry confuses prosaic minds, and music conveys no codable message, nevertheless their sound holds the mind, their forms move the heart, and what they say sinks into the soul.

Speak up then, and speak clearly so that we can all hear. Most of us won't know what you're talking about, but you mustn't mind that. Language is the life blood of society, and the root of all our mental powers. These powers are only a beginning, and the purpose of much of our culture is to get beyond mere mind. But if you neglect the beginning your journey will never start. Do not let the better debar the good. Jesus, prince of redeemers, left us hundreds of sayings. No one who thinks himself above the use of mere words can be free from pride, and he who is still proud has nothing to teach.

And yet, at the end, we are reduced to silence. The silence of sleep, the silence of meditation, the silence of death. We hear little from those who know what it is to die. The ecstatic musings of the mystic speak only to those who have shared the experience. Mere noise are most of the messages which mediums claim to bring from the dead. And those who tell us their dreams are perpetually disappointed at the reception they get. For we are here at the edge of the competence of speech to communicate, and silence is the best language.

When all the myths of the world have been rehearsed, the rites enacted, the dances danced, the audience is left in the silence to gather up what they can from the feast. Few will bring back treasures from the storehouse of wisdom. But once they were even fewer, and now it begins to appear they are less few. There is in certain favored places a breakthrough of new light into the darkened world, a new movement of revelation, and it is wise to listen. Much nonsense comes in the garb of enlightenment, and sheer trickery is rife; but the ancient wisdom is being resurrected.

Listen, then, to the silence. Listen to what they say who say nothing. Open yourself to the silence within, to the Inward Light that shines in every soul. Learn in silent waiting the gift of humility, the gift of love, the gift of tongues, the gift of expressing the silence in words so that they who understand can exchange their words for the silence from which you speak. To love one another is the essence of the spiritual quest, and those who have got thus far can use the language of silence with those they love.

Let them who seek not cease until they find. And they who have found shall wonder; and those who wonder shall possess the Kingdom; and those who have possessed it shall have rest. Thus Jesus summarized the quest, the same quest which is told in all the myths I have offered. And when—and if—you find the Holy Grail, and return in silence and as a messenger from beyond—then you are a redeemer. You are one of a growing company, but a company that can spare none of its members. All of you must live wearily in the world awhile, and leave it with more hope than you brought to it. You have Jesus as your forerunner and your model. Like him you will suffer, and like him you will conquer. May God be with you.

FUNDERBURG LIBRARY
MANCHESTER COLLEGE

215
P229w